*For Beti
- hope*

"Lovely Little Places!"
The story of the prefabs at Stewards Green, Epping.

Jenny Coumbe

For Charles, with love.

Bright Pen

Visit us online at www.authorsonline.co.uk

A Bright Pen Book

Copyright © Jenny Coumbe 2009

Front Cover image by Mary Livett ©
Back Cover photo by Ken Whitbread ©

Photos and illustrations © as credited

All rights reserved. No part of this publication may be reproduced, stored in a retrieval system, or transmitted in any form or by any means, electronic, mechanical, photocopy, recording or otherwise, without prior written permission of the copyright owner. Nor can it be circulated in any form of binding or cover other than that in which it is published and without similar condition including this condition being imposed on a subsequent purchaser.

ISBN 978-07552-1121-0

Authors OnLine Ltd
19 The Cinques
Gamlingay, Sandy
Bedfordshire SG19 3NU
England

This book is also available in e-book format, details of which are available at www.authorsonline.co.uk

Introduction

Jenny Coumbe, an Epping resident since 1994, taught for many years in Primary Schools in East London.
Recently, she began to follow her interests in Family and Social History.

This booklet grew from conversations with her neighbours Bob and Olive Knight. With their help, she contacted other former residents of the prefabs at Stewards Green. Later she appealed for more information via The Forester, The Epping Forest Guardian, and organisations such as Epping Forest District Museum who were kind enough to lend her their recording equipment. She also consulted Epping Urban District Council Minutes and local papers.

Grateful thanks to the residents for all their help:

Sylvia Brown and her daughter Angela Wilkins;
Ted Thake;
Stephen Knight;
Ken and Joyce Whitbread;
Pam O'Leary and June Jones, the Barrick sisters;
Peggy Killick;
Doreen Grimwade;
Phil Berry;
Mrs JK;
Len Butcher.
Val Flack

And especially:
Bob and Olive Knight for starting things off;
Mary Batley for the wonderfully vivid sketches;
everybody who lent photographs;
Carien Kremer for her help and advice; and
Charles Richardson for all his support and encouragement.

Further acknowledgements can be found on the References pages.

Chapter One

Air Raids and After

One afternoon, in 1940, a group of lads were playing football near Lindsey Street, Epping, when they heard a low drone that gradually got louder and louder. *"... we looked up, and in the sky there were just masses of planes all shining in the sunlight, and, course, we all started cheering, OY! But all of a sudden they came out of the sky and started dive-bombing North Weald! Next thing was, the man who lived in the end house, "Dinks" Winley shouted to us to get in his shelter. I then finished up on my knees, in the doorway of his shelter, watching it. As the crow flies, it was probably no more than two miles. There were dog-fights and goodness knows what."* (25)

Another boy was in the Empire cinema with his mum, when a sign appeared on the screen, saying that the Air Raid Siren had sounded.
"... so out we got and we stood out the front. They'd bombed North Weald ... The old Spitfires came up the High Street and I can actually remember one, literally, he turned on his side and went round the Church tower!" (10)

For young boys like Stan and Ted, this was Adventure! Edith Fairman remembers that she and her friends played with an object they'd found in Lambourne Church Field, Abridge. This turned out to be an unexploded parachute mine! (23) Lots of children collected shrapnel, and some kept mementoes for many years, such as spent bullets, and even incendiary bombs with their detonators removed. But there was, of course, a dark side. The raid that so excited those boys resulted in the deaths of at least four people, with seven seriously injured. And Edith's mysterious toy killed Lieutenant Lavender, the man who later tried to make it safe.

North Weald Airfield and London itself were the main targets for enemy action:
"We used to sit on our doorstep and we could see over London [from Upshire] *all the orange glow from the Blitz, searchlights criss-crossing and barrage balloons."* (24)

There were several near misses locally. At a cricket match, *"planes were buzzing about and all at once we realised there was a German plane coming over very, very low. We all rushed and we all fell in a ditch and I lost the heel of my shoe ...Bit scary!"* (21)

Stan Osborne's elder brother had a very eventful wedding night!
"He lived in Bower Vale, backing on to the Gas Works. [A bomb] hit a sort of railing round the top, there was quite a dent in the rail...He put his gas-mask on his wife and put a wet handkerchief over his mouth and went over there to see if there was anything he could do ... There wasn't a lot of damage ... There was very little escape of gas, as far as I can remember." (25)

Mr and Mrs Halls and their young daughter Mary, of Fiddlers Hamlet, were not so lucky. Because their cottage was wooden, for safety the family used to sleep at the grandmother's brick-built house. Bombs ruined much of the village, including the Halls' cottage. Residents were temporarily taken to Home Farm. Mary was distraught:
"I woke up during the night crying. My Mum said, "What's the matter?" I said, "My guinea pigs – are they all right?" ... They were called Rusty and Dusty Brown. ... Dad went down and they were scuttling around in their hutch. We'd got a budgie, hanging in his cage on a wall, and as Dad opened the back door the budgie said, "Poor boy, Joey, Joey's a poor boy!" (19)
The Council requisitioned the Children's Cottage Homes at Coopersale to shelter the villagers until they could be re-

housed, but several of the Fiddlers Hamlet homes proved to be beyond repair.

In the following month (October 1940) came the incident that caused the greatest loss of life in the district. A large house on Palmers Hill, Sprigg's Oak, was being used as a Maternity Home for mothers-to-be evacuated from the East End. The house took a direct hit and, sadly, eight young women lost their lives. (c)

Nevertheless, most of the Epping damage during the first few years of the war consisted of ceilings, doors and windows blown out, rather than wholesale destruction. This could be alarming enough: Stan Osborne was on his way to school when all the windows of Pyne's Department Store came down, with shards narrowly missing a woman who had been window-shopping. Church's the Pork Butchers was similarly affected.
"And of course, they never put big panes of glass back in, they boarded it up and put a little window in the middle of it."
(25)

Next came the Doodlebugs (the V1s) and their nerve-wracking drone:
"In the Senior School, some of the older boy pupils were posted on the roof. Their job was to look and listen for unusual aircraft and they had to blow a long blast on the whistle when a strange plane came over. If you heard that whistle, you had to get under the desk – there was no time to get to the shelter." (25)
A similar system was in operation at Cottis' Ironworks, to prevent constant disruption to the working day:
"What used to happen was, when the siren went, everyone carried on doing their job. Now Mr Coppin used to go on top of the concrete shelter and if he heard a doodlebug coming, he used to let the chap know in the engine-room and he used

to blow the whistle. Then there was a quick scramble, because there wasn't much time." (20)

One evening, two young brothers in their bedroom heard a doodlebug approaching:
"We were looking out the window and we saw it go right past! He said, "It's got the farm!" We thought it was hitting Shaftesbury Farm; it was so low, with the flames shooting out the back. He jumped up to the window and said, "No, it's gone over." Basically, it dropped right up near Bury Road, probably about a mile away." (25)

This may have been the same night that the chapel in the Bury Lane cemetery was destroyed:
"I can remember my mother and I being under the table and my father bringing us cocoa – all the saucepans fell from the shelves in the kitchen." (22)
"Most nights it was a bit horrendous when the bombs were dropping ...We used to go under the table, and we had a little evacuee girl with us – we had to cuddle her and the dog." (12)

In August 1944, Mr H J Mead, the Surveyor for Epping Urban District Council, reported to the War Services Committee. He explained the reason why repairs due to the blast damage and falling Anti-aircraft fragments were behind schedule. It was because local builders were wanted more urgently in London, Ongar and the Epping *Rural* District, "who have been less fortunate than ourselves." (Mins)

For the rest of that year, only minor damage was reported, so that on 6th January 1945, Mr Mead could say, referring to the previous month, "We were again fortunate in having no incidents in this district." He was, of course, tempting fate.

A week later, all the windows were blown out in The Plain and Lindsey Street areas.

A month after that, a rocket landed just off Bolt Cellar Lane, and although the damage was described as minor in character, 300 houses were affected.

In March, there were two major incidents caused by long-range rockets (V2s.) (ArW)
The first was in the Bridge Hill area, where 15 casualties had to be taken to hospital. 2 houses were completely destroyed, 31 seriously damaged, and 423 affected in total. In order to cover the roofs with tarpaulin and the windows with felt within the first 48 hours, sixty builders were drafted in from Chelmsford.

In the second incident ten days later, another rocket landed between Fairfield Road and St Margaret's Hospital. This time the victims were mainly elderly men, six of whom died, as did a hospital clerk. (c) Various hospital buildings and the water tower were damaged, and nearby 1 house was destroyed, 49 seriously damaged, and 202 affected in total. The Ministry of Works in Cambridge sent an extra one hundred men to help with the emergency repairs.

By the war's end, 29 Epping civilians had been killed. Over 1,000 homes in the Urban District had been damaged, and many, due to shortages of both materials and manpower, had not been fully restored. 16 families had been rendered homeless.

In the country as a whole, by 1945 the housing stock was in poor shape. Over three million houses needed repair, and 84,000 homes had been destroyed in London during 1944 alone. Many that were still standing were sub-standard, as both building materials and labour were in short supply. Indeed, landlords/owners had seen little point in making improvements while there was still a chance that properties might be flattened.

A further factor was that a percentage of houses had been scheduled for demolition in *pre-war* slum clearance schemes. For example, in the summer of 1939, the Surveyor had reported to Epping Urban Council that 13 houses were due to be cleared. Another 8 households were over-crowded and living in "conditions [that were] very undesirable." A further 35 families had applied for Council houses. The Surveyor was already aware that problems were being stored up for the future, because, as he explained,
"Many other applications have been received from non-residents and couples waiting to get married, but have not been recorded owing to the impossibility of granting them accommodation whilst we still have such a long waiting list of families living in the district." (Mins)

The Government was acutely aware of the need for forward planning, and as early as 1943 had begun to investigate pre-fabricated units for temporary housing.
 (A fascinating explanation of this topic can be found in Greg Stevenson's book, "Palaces for the People: Prefabs in Post-war Britain," to which I am indebted.)

A prototype "Emergency Factory-made House," made mainly of sheet metal, was exhibited in the grounds of the Tate Gallery, and in May 1944, Epping's Surveyor,
Mr H J Mead went to examine it. Aesthetically, he was less than impressed, commenting that "the houses are not exactly things of beauty, nor are they likely to remain a joy forever," but nevertheless, "there is much to be said in their favour, especially for quickly housing ex-service-men." Several features needed modifying, he felt, including the internal lay-out. He was adamant that the temporary houses should be Council-owned, for two reasons. Firstly, he was not confident that the design would resist condensation and dry rot, and therefore wanted to be sure that the buildings would be regularly maintained. Secondly, he hoped to improve their appearance by grouping them around a green. After

considerable discussion, the General Purposes Committee agreed "in principle to the erection in this district of a number of such houses."

50 were applied for, but originally only 20 "emergency dwellings" were allocated. However, after further enemy action in the district, this figure was doubled.

Next to be decided was the location of the temporary bungalows. Mr Mead's initial idea was to use an area just off Centre Road. The Housing Sub-Committee suggested an acreage at Woodberry Down, owned by the Misses Frampton, because the site was level and "rather hidden away" (!) but the Framptons were unwilling to sell. In May 1945, the Committee finally settled on a field near the junction of Bower Hill and Stewards Green Road, since the land would be cheaper, shops and transport were already present nearby, and – the clincher, apparently! – "its acquisition and use would not be likely to raise a protest."

Earlier in the year Mr Mead had addressed the Epping Women's Institute on the subject of post-war housing. The West Essex Gazette reported that he "explained that Council houses in the past had very small kitchens, no out-buildings, and a kitchen range in the same room as the family lived, because no house was allowed to cost more than £350."

He showed them three new designs of permanent Council house and asked their opinions as to facilities. The ladies suggested a spare bedroom, a separate lavatory, a gas copper in the kitchen, and commented that

"although members wanted refrigerators, none thought it very necessary."

Mr Mead did not show them plans of the various styles of temporary bungalow.

There were in fact four main types of prefab:
1. The Aluminium bungalow.
2. The Arcon Mark V, made of asbestos-cement panels on a steel frame.

3. The Uni-Seco – timber-framed, asbestos-cement panels, flat roof.
4. The Tarran – steel-framed, with panels made of a mixture of Portland cement concrete and sawdust, and a pitched roof.

(The whole point of the temporary homes was that they used as little as possible of materials that were in short supply, like bricks and timber, and could be erected by people without traditional building skills.)

The various styles were erected for inspection in Cambridge and five tickets were issued, to Mr Mead himself, to two Councillors, and to representatives of the Women's Institute and the Women's Voluntary Service. When the day came, no-one attended due to "the state of the roads, illness and other causes." In the end, this did not matter, for the decision as to the type of prefab was taken at a higher level. In February 1946, Mr Mead received a telephone call from the Ministry of Works informing him that "we had now been scheduled to receive "Tarran-type" bungalows." (Mins)

The building firm Hippersons, with the help of POW labour, were contracted to lay the roads, sewers etc, whilst Messrs Rogerson of Romford were to erect the houses. Work was due to start on 1st April 1946 and the initial stage was expected to be completed by mid-June. However, bad weather caused delays. In July, the Highways Committee decided to ask Hippersons to defer completion of the road surfaces. They suspected that these would be damaged by heavy lorries when Rogersons were erecting the bungalows.

There was now a hiatus. Although some parts had been delivered to the council depot, the main elements of the prefabs could not be supplied until the autumn.

The Express and Independent reported that at least one Councillor was furious:

> "Progress on the houses at Stewards Green Road is a real disgrace," Councillor Platten told Epping UDC on Tuesday. Councillor Platten commented, "Some things like Anderson shelters were delivered to the site and I wondered whether they were for people to live in while they were waiting for the houses to be built!"

[These were actually the garden sheds.]

Eventually the concrete slab foundations were laid and the prefabs began to be erected. Mrs Peggy Killick remembers watching:

"The walls were all standing and I saw this great big crane lift the prefab part actually inside of it..."

Now, which families were going to live there?

Chapter Two

Married, but no home of their own

The housing shortage in the Epping area was already acute by the summer of 1945. Mr Mead informed the Lettings Sub-committee that, "To date there are two hundred and ninety eight applications and it is known that there will shortly be many more."

The waiting-list contained not only long-standing applicants who were living in crowded or sub-standard conditions, but also increasing numbers of ex-Service men and women who had married during the war (or who were about to.) They were returning to the district but were unable to find homes of their own.

The local paper carried an article headed:
Share Your Rooms
which appealed to people with "large, half-empty houses" to let their spare space.

The same edition (January 1946) also had a headline:
She Cannot Get a House
But Former Employers Want Her Rooms
A woman whose accommodation went with the job had been sacked, but she had refused to move out because she couldn't find anywhere else to live. (Ind)

The majority of young couples had to start married life in the homes of their in-laws. For example, Ken and Joyce Whitbread had one room in her parents' house in Charles Street. When Joyce was pregnant, they pointed out to the midwife that they had no space for a cot. The nurse's advice?
"Oh, empty one of the drawers and put it [the baby!] *in the drawer!"* (11)

Peggy Killick and her husband and son, plus his two sisters, their husbands and children were all sharing his parents' bungalow in Bridge Hill. Living at close quarters with her mother-in-law wasn't easy: *"She was real cantankerous!"* In fact, Peggy can't imagine how they all coped.

Another couple were also initially staying with parents, in Brook Road. But, as the Committee Minutes briefly explain, "Husband sleeping at North Weald owing to lack of accommodation caused by return of another ex-Service son of the parents' family."

Later on, Bob and Olive Knight had a particularly disconcerting experience. Through a work-place friend at Epping Laundry, Olive had heard that there were rooms available at an address on Bower Hill. They went to see the woman, who accepted them as tenants. They explained that they were about to marry, and offered a deposit to cover the two weeks when they would be away on honeymoon. The landlady told them that the deposit was unnecessary, as she was going to re-decorate.

"But when we came back, the rooms had already been let! We [thought we] *were on the streets until Olive's mother volunteered to put us up!"*

And so for eight months the Knights shared a small cottage in Toot Hill with Olive's parents, two adult sisters and brother. Eventually, again through word-of-mouth, they managed to find a place in Bower Vale.

"We had one room upstairs, one room downstairs, unfurnished – we thought it was great!"

They moved in during Spring 1949 and stayed there until 1953. By this time their elder son was two and, after five years, their names had finally risen to the top of the Council's waiting-list. But to their regret, they were offered a new house on the Beaconfield estate:

"It was rather crowded - everything seemed to be on top of itself there."

Once more, word of mouth came to their aid. When shopping in Ashworth's the fish-mongers, Olive mentioned her disappointment to the owner. He told one of his employees, Mrs Berry, who lived with her husband and family at Stewards Green. The two families approached the Council and arranged a swap. (14)

Even *eight years* after the war, it was still very difficult for newly-weds to find accommodation. Ted and Ena Thake married in 1953 but *"There was literally nowhere to go,"* so they too lived with her parents, in Coopersale in a big old farmhouse. Although there were no "mod cons," at least there was plenty of space. The Thakes were there for three years.

Of the interview sample, all but one couple started married life in the homes of relatives. The exception was the Grimwades, who were renting a cramped basement bed-sit in Woolwich, South London.

At least four of the families were selected as prefab tenants for health reasons. The Council had requisitioned "Inchcape," a large house in Allnutts Road, to house people who had been bombed out. Two adults of the several families living there had TB. It was obviously important that they should not be cheek-by-jowl with others, so they were offered the prefabs. Another father, who was "bronchial," was allocated a prefab so that his child would not have to sleep in the same room. One couple who were living in overcrowded accommodation were also able to strengthen their case for priority via their doctor. The wife had had a very difficult pregnancy, and so the GP sent the Housing Officer a supportive letter. (Mins)

Of course, it was very frustrating for those people who were waiting years for a house, and unsurprisingly, suspicions of favouritism sometimes arose.
An Express and Independent article in May 1946 provides an example:

Requisitioned house freed for ex-Serviceman to buy
"OTHER FAMILIES LIVING IN WORSE CONDITIONS" –
Assert Councillors

> While some small cottages in Epping are occupied by ten people, a house in Bury Road, formerly requisitioned by the council, has been sold to a married couple – and some members of Epping Urban District Council think it is wrong.
> [..........]
> Coun. Pring asked: "If we have a points scheme for allocating houses, why don't we stick to it?"
> Coun. Mrs Lamb commented: [......] The Ministry of Health say that it is not our duty as a local authority to interfere with the normal sale of property. We are not expected to solve our housing problem by requisitioning but by building new houses."

The response of the Housing and War Services Committee to the furore was to hold a Special Meeting in July. It was decided that the application forms should not have names and addresses of applicants on, just a number, and that the selection of tenants should be made from the form information alone. The process had not only to *be* fair, it had to be *seen* to be fair.

Nevertheless, just a few months later, the paper was reporting another disagreement:

Epping Housing Controversy
WHY COUNCILLORS RESIGNED FROM COMMITTEE

Councillor Gouldstone and Miss Hart had resigned because:
> "two persons who were living outside the district, but who previously resided within the Council area,

were given priority on the question of a new house." (Ind Jan 1947)

The waiting applicants frequently went to the Council Offices in person, to chivvy the Housing Officers and to check their position on the lists. For example, Olive Knight reckons she went once or twice a month.

When their daughter was three, and they were still in their Woolwich basement, the Grimwades sent a strong letter to the Council, which seemed to have the desired effect. Mrs Grimwade thought that *"...they forgot us because we were out of the area."*

The first twelve families were notified that they were allocated to the Stewards Green prefabs in November 1946, and by May 1947 all the bungalows were occupied. All had at least one family member born or brought up in Epping, and the majority contained one or more children. Mrs JK and her husband, for instance, were both Epping people; he had spent a full six years in the Navy; they had a baby son; they had been living with her parents, who were also housing relatives who had been bombed out of Bridge Hill. As a result, they *"got enough points to have a 'fab straight away."*

(Transcripts of the first scheme for selecting tenants in Temporary Houses and the original Housing Application Form are on pages 20, 21 and 22, and one of the original notification letters is on page 23.)

The almost immediate popularity of prefabs in general is shown by the Electricity advertisement from "Illustrated" magazine, reproduced on page 19. The advertiser is associating the prefab with modern technology, and the newly-housed young woman is told that it's her lucky day. Clearly, many Stewards Green residents felt the same (although *their* kitchens had gas appliances, not electric.). In the December of that first full year, 31 of the original families became eligible for *permanent* houses. They received a letter from the Council which asked them for their housing preference. Almost half of them chose not to move, and several other families, later, also decided to stay put. Clearly, there was something about Stewards Green!

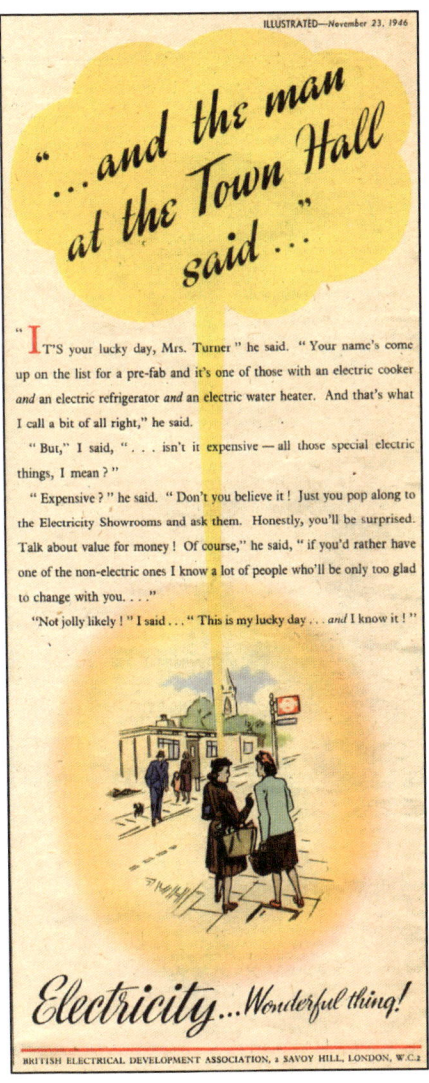

(Thanks to Gordon and Elizabeth Dent)

"SCHEME for priorities in the selection
of Tenants for Temporary and Requisitioned Houses."

THE persons eligible for temporary or requisitioned houses are those who have resided in Epping Urban District at any time up to the cessation of hostilities in September 1945.

POINTS shall be awarded by the Letting Committee to applicants in accordance with the Schedule below.

APPLICANTS will be permitted to occupy houses as and when they become ready for occupation in the order ascertained by the award of points.

THE SCHEDULE

	Points	Maximum
H. M. FORCES MERCHANT NAVY & WAR WORKERS		
(1) For Service abroad – for each year or part of a year	5 }	
(2) " " at home - " "	4 }	30
(3) War Workers " "	4 }	
HOMELESS (From whatever cause)		
(1) By enemy action	25 }	
(2) Eviction	20 }	25
(3) Never had home	20 }	
CHILDREN		
For each child aged 16 or under	4	20
HEALTH		
Overcrowding (Statutory) or	}	
Condemned property or	}	15
Very bad conditions (in the opinion of the Sanitary Inspector)	}	
LOCAL RESIDENCE		
For each full year of residence in the Urban Area prior to September 1945 (either husband or wife)	1	10
		100
SELECTION COMMITTEE AWARD		
The Committee may in exceptional cases award additional points up to a maximum of		10

EPPING URBAN DISTRICT COUNCIL
HOUSING APPLCATION FORM   NO………..

NAME OF APPLICANT ……………………………………..AGE ……

PRESENT ADDRESS ………………………………………………………..
(For the purpose of communications in
connection with this application.) ………………………………………………..

PARTICULARS OF WAR SERVICE   yrs   mths
1. Length of Service in Gt Britain. …………………………….
                                              Total Service ……………..
2.   "   "   Overseas. ……………………………
3.   "   "   as War Worker with ………………………..
here give Employer's name and address
………………………………………………………………………………..
………………………………………………………………………………..
Nature of Employment ……………………………………………………….
4.   Service No. and Unit ……………………………………………
5.   If wholly or partially disabled through War Injury give brief particulars.
………………………………………………….

PRESENT POSITION WITH REGARD TO A HOME
Have you   Strike out words not applicable
1. Been rendered homeless by enemy action   Yes   No
If answer is "Yes" give name and address of house.
………………………………………………………………………………
………………………………………………………………………………
2. Been evicted   Yes   No
If answer is "Yes" give brief reason here …………………………………..
………………………………………………………………………………
3. Never had a home.   Yes   No

PARTICULARS OF FAMILY

ADULTS	CHILDREN
Male Female	Age Sex

PRESENT ACCOMMODATION
Address where now living if different from No. 2.
………………………………………………………………………………….
………………………………..
No. of Rooms and Approximate Size

Nature of Room i.e. Lvg or Bed.	Approx Size

P.T.O

-21-

LENGTH OF RESIDENCE IN EPPING

No. of years	Address at which most of this time was spent.
Husband	....
Wife	....

NAME AND ADDRESS OF PRESENT OR INTENDED EMPLOYER
....
....
    1. How long have you been in his employ? ……………………………..
    2. Position held or nature of work ………………………………………

PRESENT RENT PAID ....(Per Week)

PRESENT LANDLORD'S NAME AND ADDRESS
....
....

WHAT APPROXIMATE WEEKLY (INCLUSIVE) RENT CAN YOU AFFORD?
....

NAME AND ADDRESSES OF TWO PERSONS WHO WILL (IF REQUIRED) SPEAK AS TO YOUR CHARACTER AND SUITABILITY AS A TENANT.
....
....

OBSERVATIONS – Applicants may set out below (not in separate letters) any further particulars they may wish to add in support of their applications.

This form when completed should be returned to:-
The Council Offices,
91, High Street   Epping.

Epping Urban District Council.

Tel. No. EPPING 2256/7

Hawthorn Lodge,
91 High Street,
Epping, Essex.

5th December, 1946.

Dear Sir,

I am now able to inform you that you have been allocated a prefabricated house on the Stewards Green Estate. At the moment I cannot tell you exactly which house you will be occupying, nor the date when it will become available to you. It is hoped that all will be ready by the end of January and as much notice as possible will be given you of the exact house you are to occupy and the date when it will be ready for you.

The weekly rent for these houses is £1. payable in advance and the money will be called for on Tuesday mornings by the Council's Collector, Miss . Green.

I must also draw your attention to the fact that as outbuildings will be provided by the Council no other sheds or buildings will be allowed to be erected on this Estate.

In order to assist all tenants in getting the best possible use out of the electric and other appliances in these houses, arrangements have been made for a Ministry of Fuel Demonstrator to be present from 2 p.m. to 4 p.m. on Tuesday next the 10th inst. This Demonstrator will be in one of the nearly completed houses on the Estate and you are strongly advised to visit this house during this time in order that you may learn as much as possible of the manner in which the various appliances should be used. In this way you will be able to get the maximum results with the minimum of running cost to yourselves.

For your further information all houses on the Estate are of exactly the same size and you will be allowed into any of them for the purpose of measuring for lino and curtains on presentation of this letter to the Clerk of Works or the Foreman in charge.

Yours faithfully,

H.J. Mead,
Survsyor & Sanitary Inspector.

(Thanks to Mary Batley)

Chapter Three

<u>All Mod Cons</u>

The first thing the new residents would have appreciated was the uncrowded aspect of the estate. Each prefab was essentially a small detached bungalow sitting in its own garden, separated from its neighbour by about 8 feet and a chain-link fence. This ensured that there was *"sufficient space so that we couldn't hear what was being said in the prefab next door!"* (8)

Fourteen of the prefabs were arranged in a U shape, backing on to a green open area, while the rest were arranged in an outer circle. The frontages were not in a straight line but were subtly staggered. This layout was no doubt due to Mr Mead, the Council's Surveyor, and contrasts favourably with some of the larger prefab estates, which looked like regimented rows of uniform boxes.

Adapted from a plan produced by the Council, prior to redevelopment.

The Tarran bungalows were the heaviest of the various prefab types and had a solid appearance. It was just possible, therefore, to imagine them as country cottages. Indeed, outside her back bedroom Mrs Killick built a rose arbour:
"I used to go over the field and get lots of bits of wood ... I twisted them all in and out and then I covered it with every type of climbing rose." (7)

(courtesy Len Butcher)

The wall panels were of "Lignocrete" with a pebble-dashed finish – *"They were so pretty, they had all those lovely little stones on the outside"* – and the roofs were shallow-pitched corrugated asbestos sheets. There was a path up to the central front door and *"a really wide side walk round to the back door so you didn't have to take your prams and so on through the inside."* (7)

The front of the prefab at night.
(Thanks to Mary Batley)

The estate was separated from Stewards Green Road by a straggly hedge and more chain-link fencing. In 1947, Mr Mead suggested planting standard trees along the hedge-line to improve the appearance. The following spring, twenty trees were planted, a mixture of Norway Maple, Sycamore, Poplar and Lime, only two of which remain today.

Along the eastern boundary was a stream that fed into the brook. Beyond it and on the other sides were fields:
"We had nobody - just fields - around us. It was an absolutely idyllic spot. We had such a lot of wildlife, so many birds and rabbits and hedgehogs. We had a pond in the field, because the cattle used to water in the fields, and we had the lovely big protected newts in it ... it really was a lovely spot." (3)

"It really was a lovely spot." (L B)

It is easy to forget that for many families, household amenities had barely improved during the first half of the 20th century. It was common, especially in rural districts, for cottages to have *"no water, no electric light and the toilet outside – terrible really, but we were used to all that."* (9)

Builders of *new* homes were not obliged to lay on water until the passing of the 1945 Water Act, which stipulated that: "Instead of plans providing for the supply of water in, *or within a reasonable distance of the houses,* [my emphasis] they must propose to connect the house with the supply provided by a local authority or other water undertaker, or failing this, must take the water into the house by means of a pipe."

(From a draft of the Act.)

Things changed slowly. Even in the early 1950s many people still had very limited facilities, as can be gathered from this article in the Epping edition of the Express and Independent:

Old Houses May Get Hot Water
"Epping UDC are to consider improvements to pre-war houses. When the Council met on Tuesday, Mr JG Lusty said they were considering providing electric light and hot water systems in these houses."

[Feb 1953]

Note the date, and the words *may* and *considering!*

Many of the tenants who came to Stewards Green would therefore have been used to fairly basic facilities. Toilets were often outside. For example, pre-war at Epping Green, Mrs Brown's family lived in *"a tiny cottage with the toilet at the end of the garden,"* while at Fiddlers Hamlet the Halls had *"quite a walk, it seemed to me, up the garden to go to the toilet"* which consisted of a *"bucket-and-chuck-it"* system.
(18)

Bath night loomed large in several people's childhood memories:

"The bath came out on Friday evenings, when the youngest used it first, and then we progressed through until Dad ended up being the last one in front of the fire." (8)

Ken Whitbread recalls a similar scene from his Lindsey Street days:
"We had the old tin bath that was brought in front of the fire ...we all queued up."
This would have taken quite a time as there were eight children in the family!

The Whaleys' house in Charles Street did have a bathroom, but it was *"downstairs next to the back door ...We were so surprised* [on moving in] *because you had a lid that you had to lift up before you could have a bath."* (12)

When the Knights were staying with their in-laws, post-war, at Toot Hill,
"We had a tin bath in the wood shed, which was called the washing shed, where the copper was. We had to go down the road with a 10-gallon churn to fill up with water at the tap at Pledge's Farm, wheel it back on this little trolley, tip it into the copper, and while it was warming up, go and get another one. And hopefully, the water would still be there when you got back! On one day, the shed door was locked! Olive's sister had stolen my bath water!" (8)

On moving to their two rooms in Bower Vale, Epping, they still had no bathroom, though water was laid on. So they were delighted when they arrived in the prefab to find that *"we had our own bathroom, we had a separate toilet inside, we had hot and cold water taps in the bathroom and in the kitchen! Luxury!"* (8 and 9)

Peggy Killick was also impressed with the prefab bathroom: *"By the head of the bath there was a piece of wood that pulled up, with a bracket underneath, like a very strong little triangular table. It was so useful for drying the babies and putting their nappies on, and you could keep an eye on the one who was still in the bath. Or when you were cleaning the bath, you could stand your gear on it. You had everything at your fingertips."* (This may have been unique to this particular prefab.)

Prefab bath-time (L B)

(M B)

There is no doubt that the prefabs' outstanding feature was the fully equipped kitchen. Adjectives like "thrilled!" "wonderful" and "out of this world!" pepper the interviews, for as well as hot and cold water and electric light, a gas copper *and* a gas refrigerator were fitted as standard. (Only one year previously, the Epping Women's Institute had told Mr Mead that fridges were wanted but were not "very necessary". Indeed, many households, including my own, didn't have one until twenty years later.)

In fact, so futuristic did these kitchens seem that the Council doubted whether residents would know how to use them, as this 1946 report to the Housing and War Services Committee makes clear:

"Fitments: Attention has been drawn to the importance of offering continual assistance and advice in regard to the use of those dwellings – particularly the kitchen unit – and arrangements are being made, first for a demonstrator from the Ministry of Fuel and Power to explain to the tenants the object and use of the various fittings, and, secondly, for the rent collector to be instructed in such matters that she may be in a position to advise tenants." (Mins)

Apparently, "all the existing and most of the prospective tenants" attended the demonstration in the following January, but none of the interviewees were there.

People's wide-eyed amazement at the modernity can still be heard all these years later:

"I can remember Mum and Dad being really pleased to move into the prefabs because they had these lovely fitted kitchens ... You'd got it all compact with nice working surfaces ... Mum was thrilled!" (5)

"Then there was a pantry with ventilation ... and that was absolutely huge, you could walk in that." (3)

The kitchen (M B)

"We even had a gas refrigerator, which was out of this world! Ice creams and all that sort of stuff! And then, beside the sink we had a gas boiler with a wringer over the top so you could get [the washing] straight out and put it through the wringer. We had a gas stove with a gas grill above it, and loads of cupboard space below the work surface, which was all down one side of the kitchen ...We were in clover!" (8)

"A [work] top came down that washed off and was all clean, and everything pushed away. Now I think that was very neat, absolutely neat!" (7)

"… you could get the washing straight out …" (L B)

-32-

"The kitchen table you didn't have to buy, because there was one in the kitchen that [folded] up and during the day it went down." (11)

The folding table (L B)

The amount of cupboard space was also a revelation:

"Every bit of furniture that you could possibly need was built in ... They always mirrored what was on the other side, so you'd get cupboards and drawers on the lounge side, cupboards and drawers on the kitchen side ...They were all made out of pressed metal .. ." (3)

The metal bedroom cupboards   (JMC, Eden Camp Museum.)

"Even the airing cupboard was nicely built, in a space where it didn't interfere with anything." (11)

The one innovation that did not meet with universal approval was the "hot air" method of heating the bedrooms. Opinions differed widely as to its efficacy.
First, the approvers:
"You only had one fire and that was in the sitting-room. The heat used to go up into funnels that used to go along the ceilings and into the bedrooms and everywhere, so the house was always warm." (11)
"We used to have a lovely fire ... The fire was one of those lovely little ones where the doors shut on, and a raised front." (7)

-33-

The Livetts' bedroom at No.34, with imitation-parquet lino. (M B)

Colin's bedroom, No 34. (M B)

Living-room, showing the fire. (M B)

On the other hand:
"The fire that we had burnt coke or anthracite. From there, there were heat ducts going into both bedrooms and also the hallway. They weren't all that efficient, so what we did, we had a paraffin heater." (8)

And Doreen Grimwade was not at all impressed! The window-frames of her prefab were not a tight fit. As a result, the fringe on her cotton carpet *"used to flap about when it got really windy!"* And during the winter, *"Whatever the temperature was <u>outside</u>, that was the temperature <u>inside</u>! They never retained any heat at all ... The bedrooms were so cold, you'd go to bed with mittens and woolly hats on!"*

Similarly, *"When there was a bad frost, I remember the ice was inside the windows. Mum would put some hot water in a stone water bottle and put it in her bed."* (13)

A member of the Epping Housing Department confirms that, *"we used to get a few complaints (from some tenants) about the dampness and how much it cost them to heat the properties. But not that many."* (25)

(Of course, it is only comparatively recently that it has become normal to heat bedrooms. Until the last 20 years or so of the 20th century, "Jack Frost" ice patterns on the insides of windows were common, even in permanent houses.)

The Barrick sisters remembered the opposite problem: *"Because the summers were exceptionally hot, sometimes Dad, of an evening, would throw down buckets of cold water onto the stones to try and help the building cool down a bit, because the sun was still beating down on the windows of our bedroom."* (5)

Pam and June were very fond of their *"light and airy"* room, a quality mentioned by others, too. The bedroom window was over half the length of its wall, and both the kitchen and the sitting-room had two windows, so there was plenty of natural light: *"Lovely windows, nice and light it was."* (6)

showing the corner window. (M B)

Living-room, (M B)

When the residents first moved in, *"the walls were a biscuit colour and the doors were cream."* Mary Batley's sketches show how their front room looked after her mother had redecorated the walls with "Sunlight Yellow" distemper.

"The bright yellow went lovely with my Mum's green shining lino and her green Rexene two-seater settee and armchair." (13)

The other aspect which delighted people was the well-proportioned rooms:

The kitchen had enough space *"for us to sit and have our breakfast altogether."* (5)

"All the rooms were almost square, a nice shape." (12)

On the next page is a plan of the Tarran Mark 4 Temporary House, adapted from a Ministry of Works document dated 1943. (My drawing's scale is approximate.)

Note how the plumbing and heating arrangements back on to each other. This canny design was known as the "heart unit." The bedrooms were both 11 feet 9 inches by 10ft 2ins, while the sitting room was a generous 14ft 11ins by 10ft 2ins.

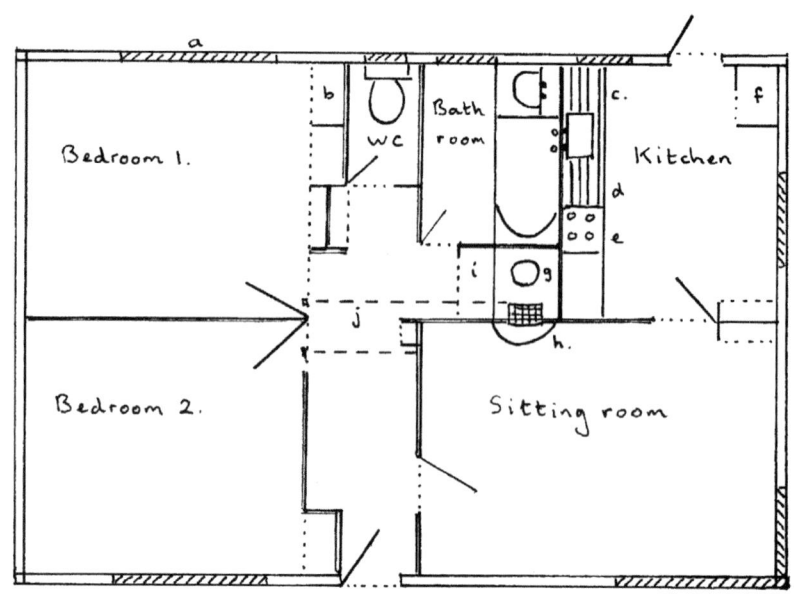

Key
a) windows b) cupboards c) gas refrigerator d) copper e) oven, hob and grill f) larder g) hot water cylinder h) fire – stove boiler i) airing cupboard j) hot-air ducts

To end the chapter, here is a selection of the very positive over-all comments that the prefabs inspired:
"Lovely little places!" (1)
"Well thought-out." (11)
"It really was beautifully designed – ideal!" (3)
"Whoever designed those, they deserved a medal, they really did!" (7)

Step forward **C J Mole** of the Ministry of Works and **A W Kenyon**, Consultant Architect, who were responsible for the prototype from which all prefabs developed, and the anonymous designer(s) who worked for Robert Tarran at **Tarran Industries** in Hull.

Chapter Four

Making Ends Meet

In the immediate post-war years, hundreds of thousands of ex-Service personnel across the country were being re-absorbed into the employment market. Some sank thankfully back into "Civvy Street" and their old ways of life. Some had learnt new skills in the Forces and hoped to use them; others had these hopes dashed. There were also wounded men coming to terms with the limiting effects of their injuries.

Each category had at least one representative on the Stewards Green estate:
Ted Thake (after 3 years' "Duration of Present Emergency" service in the RAF) was happy to go back to Pyne's Department Store in Epping High Street, being by nature *"a contented soul."* No longer "the lad," he gradually began to climb the firm's ladder, eventually running the Menswear Department.

Ken Whitbread, however, did not want to go back to being a butcher for the Co-op. During his time in the RAF he had teamed up with a friend, taking portrait photos for the men to send back to wives and girlfriends. On return, after a short while in his old occupation, he set himself up in business as a professional photographer.

Not everyone was so fortunate. Bob Knight had hoped to do *"what I had done in the Navy, and that was radio communications,"* so he went to Marconi's at North Weald. There he was told to apply to Electra House on the Embankment.
"I had the interview and got accepted, but had to go on a waiting list because of all the people coming out of the Forces. And I thought, I can't live like this ..."

He was despondent and found solace down the pub. Word-of-mouth came to his rescue, for a friend there told him there was a vacancy for a porter at Epping Station. He got the job and thoroughly enjoyed working on the railways. During the prefab years he became a signalman. Later, he went into management.

Olive Barnes (later Knight) had volunteered for the Army partly to get away from the drudgery of domestic work. She had been in the Radar section of an Anti-aircraft unit and had also briefly driven supply trains. But after demobilisation,
"It was terrible to come back, because there was nothing, really, at Toot Hill."
She started work at Epping Laundry *"because there wasn't much else."* This involved *"packing, labelling, sorting – all boring, boring, boring!"*
She was glad to leave when her first son was born.

In contrast, Mrs JK, who had been directed into Epping Laundry as her contribution to the war effort, was more than happy to go back once her son was old enough:
"I loved it. I was on the press, and [loved] to see those white coats coming out all perfect!"

Peggy Killick's husband Jack had a difficult time. He had spent five years in a POW camp in Poland and had returned with frost-bitten hands and feet. As a result, at first he could only manage two or three days work a week. Things were very tight, so the recently-introduced Family Allowance for the second child became vital: *"Sometimes I was waiting, worse than waiting, for that 8 shillings ...just to get a meal."*

The rent for each prefab was £1 a week, including the water rate and general rate. Miss Green, the Council rent collector, *"would knock on the door with her satchel on. We had a rent card, which we would hand over with the money. She would*

sign the rent card and hand it back to you with any change. Then she'd say, "I'll see you next week." (8)
Alternatively, people went up Bower Hill to the Housing Offices in the High Street – Mrs Grimwade, for example, a full-time teacher, paid her rent there monthly.

The Knights had previously been paying 14 shillings for two rooms with few facilities, so they considered the prefab rent to be good value, even though it represented almost 40% of Bob's basic pay. With his overtime, that *"still left a reasonable living amount. It was supplemented by potato-picking in the field on the other side [of the estate] where Mr Scadding used to grow potatoes. He used to pay us 4d a bag, I think it was ... You'd pick a hundred-weight of potatoes up. The first day was wonderful. It was the morning of the second day when you noticed that you'd got a back-ache!"* (Others remember it being 9d a bag, and as can be seen in the photo on the next page, this rose to 1 shilling.)

At weekends, men, women and children from the estate and from the Ivy Chimneys area would be recruited into the fields. During the week, many of the women, most of whom were housewives, would take further advantage of the seasonal work.

Mary Batley recalls that *"In 1950, my mum would take me on the fields and Mrs Hawes would take her son Anton. All four of us would walk to the bottom of the main road near the prefabs and wait for the lorry driven by Mr Smith. The lorry was packed with women and push-chairs. All the women wore head-scarves round their hair and some wore trousers with bib-fronts. My mum Lily Livett and myself would sit with the driver in his cab."* (13)

Mary and Mrs Hawes (M B)

Peggy Killick remembers that the farmer arrived with tractor and trailer to collect the ladies. They went to the farms of *"various Padfields and Mr Donaldson at Fiddlers Corner."* Once they were at their destination, *"You had so many sacks dumped, and the tractor came along the length of the field throwing up the potatoes all the time ...There'd be four of you on one row and then there'd be a gap, and then some more ... You'd get no more than 9d, and you had to fill the sack right to the top."*

On one occasion a certain farmer was being awkward about payment:

"We didn't finish the field because he wouldn't pay the extra penny or two on it, so we flung down his sacks and said, That's it!"

Although it was back-breaking work, Mrs Killick thoroughly enjoyed it:
"At midday you'd sit down with your flask and all sit round in a circle and everybody would talk to everybody else. You forgot you'd been a bit depressed the day before ...
I used to save up that potato-picking money and I used to guard it – I had such plans for it!"

"At midday..." Mrs Edney, Mary Livett, Mrs Hawes and Anton, Lily Livett, unknown.   (MB)

Doreen Grimwade recalls that the pea-picking day started really early:
"You'd get to the peas and the dew would still be on them – you'd get soaked!"

A perk of the farm work was the chance of extras:
"... all the potatoes hidden in the prams underneath, not the ones he let us have, the ones hid in the prams! He knew they were there but he never used to say anything, because all the farmers were really pleased to have us." (7)

Even after a potato field had been harvested, it could still provide a few meals:

"The farmer used to come up at night-times and we'd all be out there gleaning, picking up what was left. Everybody on the estate would be out there with their wheel-barrows and sacks. He said we had more potatoes off his field than he got!" (11)

These were well worth having, because potatoes were rationed for the first time in November 1947.

Employers would sometimes approach residents directly:

"Mr Fradd came to the door and said, "Would you like a job ...in a nursery?" I said I didn't know one plant from another!" (9)

Nevertheless, Olive and her friend started work at Shallsmere Nursery, Stapleford Tawney, and Olive did two or three days a week for the next 12 years. Mr Fradd used to pick them up in the morning and dropped them back in the afternoon. The job mainly entailed disbudding and *"potting the tiny seeds you prick out – I used to do a hundred boxes a day."* An advantage was that her sons could come with her during the school holidays: *"There was a river running through so they used to go fishing ... we'd take a picnic with us."* (9)

Similarly, Mr Mark Lemon of Epping Laundry personally asked Mrs JK to return.

Residents' occupations were quite varied and included: agricultural workers; bakery rounds-man; building tradesmen; bus-driver; butcher; cabinet-maker; cleaning ladies; drivers; electrician; engineer; handyman; house-wives; nursery workers; painter-and-decorators; plumber; photographer; servicemen; seamstress; school dinner lady; shop-workers; signalman; teacher; window-cleaner and so on. Some people who had a special skill would use it to earn a bit of extra cash. For instance, one man used to cut people's hair for them. (18)

Most households had only one full-time wage-earner. Also, for the first six post-war years, some food-stuffs were still rationed and coupons were still needed for clothes, furniture and furnishings. And so, like everyone else, the Stewards Green residents had to show ingenuity and resourcefulness in order to make ends meet.

As has already been shown, they counted themselves as fortunate because much of the necessary furniture and fittings were provided:
"You didn't have to buy anything! It was absolutely brilliant!" (3)
This was an exaggeration, but demonstrates people's enthusiasm for the fitments.
"You didn't have to worry about cupboards ... Luckily, we did manage to get a bedroom suite. Somebody was moving and they'd got one to sell – it was a very good hand-made one. We had to buy a couch and a three-piece suite ..." (11)
"We had no furniture, nothing, we had literally nothing, and I will say that's where my mother-in-law helped out. She used to go to the Loughton Auction Rooms and buy odds and ends for us." (7)

In the early days, the only brand-new furniture available was from the "Utility" range – a thrifty and straightforward style that was for a long time denigrated, but now has its admirers.

Soft furnishings were also in short supply, so people did what they could:
"Our first mats ... My husband and I used to get sugar sacks and open them. We used to get all sorts of different kinds of bits of rags, cut them into strips, a great pile of them, sharp down a peg till it had a point and we used to put [the strips] through ... That was our first carpets and they lasted for years – they looked really nice." (7)

Replica rag rug, made by Peggy Killick in 2008.

"The windows had no nets, just three strips of curtains that had been threaded through stretch wire". (13)
"I didn't have any curtains at all when I moved in. Then I just had curtains that didn't draw, that was the next step. Then eventually we got proper curtains." (3)

Curtains were the first thing that Peggy Killick bought with her carefully-guarded potato-picking money. After that, it went towards fuel for the fire:

"[The coalman] couldn't always deliver. I used to push this old truck up to the Gas Works. You could go and get a hundredweight of coke. They'd weigh it up for you, it was a pound, and I'd go up five times ... That would last me for a long time."

Sylvia Brown also recalls going up to the station with a barrow to collect coal. She remembers that, when the prefabs were brand new, there was a problem about where to store fuel: *"[Someone] used to have the coal shot in their bedroom!"*

There was a good reason for this, as was reported in the local paper:

"Coal in my bedroom"
Epping prefab occupiers' complaint

> "Tenants at the prefab site in Stewards Green Road, Epping, are having to store coal in their bedrooms because no coal storage accommodation has been built by Epping Urban District Council.
>
> Mrs E. B. told the "Express and Independent" that coal, allowed to her to "air-off" her newly occupied prefab, had to be dumped in the back bedroom …
>
> "We are afraid of having it pinched if we leave it in the open."
>
> But Mrs A. B is taking a chance on her coal vanishing.
>
> "I am leaving it in the open," she said. "We have had shelters lying dismantled in our back gardens for weeks now. We were told they could not be erected because the Council wanted to level the ground … but they could have been put up at least temporarily, saving us taking a chance when fuel is so scarce."
>
> (Ind. 22.2.47)

This was no joke. Severe winter weather, that had started at the end of January 1947 and lasted until March, coincided with difficulties with extracting and transporting enough coal. Many people collected dead wood from the local countryside to keep their fires going, a custom that continued.

Wooding (L B)

In August 1947, Prime Minister Clement Attlee warned that Britain was struggling to pay for imported goods. As a result, food rations were cut. Indeed, the meat ration was reduced *three times* between the end of the war and 1951. However, (as depicted on TV's "Dad's Army") some people had useful contacts! One resident remembers,

"As far as meat was concerned I was very lucky ...I went down to the butchers right down the bottom of the town ... I gave this [bloke] our ration books ... Oh, he said, you're married to one of the Xs are you? I said, All depends!"

It turned out that he was a pre-war friend of her husband's and so often allowed her extra offal. *"Isn't it strange, doesn't matter what it is, you get a fiddle, don't you!"*

Backyard hens, which had been a mainstay of both country folk and town dwellers during the war years, came into their own again. (Just one *bought* egg was allowed per person per week.) Here are the Barrick sisters' memories:

"The chickens were at the back of the garden, with the chicken-house and the chicken-run. We always had a cockerel to look after the hens, possibly six or eight hens. Mum always used to have two or three that she would fatten up ready for Christmas, for us and perhaps for Nan and family." (5)

"She used to cook big containers – potato peelings and everything – mix them all up, and then bang the tin and they all came running!" (4)

"Yes, she would make a mash with bran for them. We used to break up sea-shells because that helped them to produce the egg-shells." (5)

"When Mum was ready for one of the hens, [Bunny the Butcher] would come along and kill it for her." (4)

The Whitbreads also had six hens.
"The cockerel used to stalk me! I was frightened to go in the garden. He used to really go for me!" (12)
Joyce would take a broom with her for protection!

At least two other families kept hens for their eggs and meat. One household made absolutely sure that their chickens were safe overnight by using the second bedroom as the hen-house. (Info from 1)

The war-time "Dig for Victory" campaign had seen many grand gardens turned over to food production, including the Tower of London's moat and part of Kew Gardens. Locally, a golf course was ploughed up and planted. The wish to be as self-sufficient as possible seems to have sent down deep roots - everybody in my interview sample grew at least some of their own vegetables, and a few had fruit bushes and fruit trees, too:

"Potatoes, beetroot, tomatoes, parsnips, carrots, blackcurrants, apples – [we grew] everything!" (11 and 12)

"We had quite a reasonable size garden – some was a lawn with flower beds and behind that we had the vegetables. We *[three sisters] all had a little patch to cultivate of our own ... so we were learning about growing things. It was usually potatoes and runner beans, blackcurrant and raspberry canes, gooseberry bushes."* (4 and 5)

"The gardens were beautiful ... Mind you, it was thick heavy clay. My husband enjoyed his gardening, so by the time he'd been there churning it over year after year and digging in the compost, roses and apple trees grew like mad ... We grew everything in the garden, all the soft fruits – strawberries, gooseberries, blackcurrants, vegetables – and [we had] this patch of grass that my husband dutifully mowed." (3)

The Anderson-shelter sheds were handily placed for storing garden tools, being just outside the back door. (They also housed kindling, paraffin, and also bikes and toys.)

Shed   (courtesy Bob and Olive Knight.)

People also made use of the adjoining countryside:
"My husband had some ferrets, because in those days, rabbits was a meal and of course the disease wasn't about, so you didn't have to worry. He went out with a mate across the road. They used to go out in their spare time, when they could, so we always had a meal. [The rabbit] was either roast, boiled, or baked ... they kept us going, they really did." (7)

Blackberrying was popular, and some people also collected mushrooms and sweet chestnuts from fields on the edge of Gaynes Park or from the Ivy Chimneys area.
June Jones recalls that their chestnuts were roasted over the sitting-room fire, using a pan made out of dried-baby-milk tins, with a long wire handle.

As well as her mother making jam, chutneys and fruit pies, Pam O'Leary remembers that: *"My Dad used to make home-made wine. That's one of the reasons we used to go and pick the sloes and elderberries. Different neighbours and family would come over and they had to have a little taste of the latest one to see what they thought. They used to discuss recipes at work and with friends, and pass on ones that had been successful ... wheat wine, sloe wine, sloe gin, and blackberry, they were some of the most popular ones. Suddenly, sometimes, in warm weather, you'd get an explosion and everything smelt a bit "winey" for a few days! Mum would say, "Jim, you can't do it there any more! You're not putting that in my airing cupboard!"*

Although rationing and shortages continued into the early 1950s, things across the country were gradually improving. The beginning of the National Health Service in 1948, more extensive welfare provision and almost full male employment meant that the disposable incomes of most households increased slowly but steadily. This would have been true for the majority of Stewards Green residents, too.

Chapter 5

Round and About

As has been mentioned, Stewards Green was chosen for the prefab site *because* it was comparatively isolated. To get to the High Street was (and is) a stiff walk of almost a mile which rises steeply through about 180 feet (60 metres.) The residents seemed to take this in their stride, as most were young and fit.

The 381 service was not introduced until 30th August 1950. The new bus travelled along Fiddlers Road past Stewards Green, connecting Toot Hill and Mount End with the station and the town. There were five departures in each direction every weekday, and a single fare from Epping to the end of the route at the Green Man cost sixpence. Here is how the local paper described the first day:

First Bus runs to Toothill

Women shoppers make most of new service

"Early on Wednesday morning eight passengers climbed aboard a new green bus standing at Epping LT Garage, the driver took his seat, and away went the first bus on the new Epping to Toothill route.

This was the last chapter in a history of long negotiation with London Transport for the provision of the service.

Most of the first eight passengers were women shoppers. The driver was Mr J Walker of Harlow. The route is No. 381 and the coaches are 20-seaters."

It was also reported that "crowds of shoppers travelled on the bus making the return trip at lunch-time on Wednesday." (E and I)

However, only one of the Stewards Green interviewees used the bus regularly, when she combined going to work with taking her daughter to school. She recalls that *"all the drivers were very good"* (1) and knew all the children. Another person remembers a driver being very kind to her mother. She realised that she had dropped her purse at the stop, so the driver turned the bus around and went back to look for it. (18)

It was more common for the women to *"trudge up the hill with the pram"* (8) because *"we were so used to walking then."* (9)

"There was a bus, if you could afford it, but getting a push-chair on, and a little tot, and your shopping ..." (7)

Typical London Country buses (M B)

It wasn't absolutely necessary to go up to the High Street for food. Although some people preferred to shop at the Co-op, the International Stores, Harrison's the Greengrocer, Church's the Butcher, etc, others used the *"four shops all within a few minutes of one another."* (5) Mrs Barrick, for instance, did most of her shopping at Dingley's in Allnutts Road and Weller's in Brook Road, supplemented by the Monday market.

Dingley's (which housed a sub-Post Office) sold general provisions: tins, dried goods (such as rice, semolina, flour,) packets of biscuits, and bacon. If you asked for bacon, *"he would religiously cut the rind off before putting it in the machine to cut into rashers."* (8)

(M B)

Weller's was also a general store selling food and household goods, including kindling and firelighters. *"On Sundays I would push my doll's pram up to do the shopping for Mum."* (13) It sold beer, wines and spirits, as well as Tizer, lemonade, and so on. Children would take back empty bottles *"to get thruppence or whatever to buy sweets."* (2) Mrs Brown particularly liked the sausages she bought there. These were probably supplied by Billy Lawrence, who lived in a bungalow in Sunnyside Road.

"He had a big shed where he would sit all day and make sausages for half-a-crown a pound. I remember Billy walking along Brook Road with a big, heavy basket of sausages under his arm. Billy was bandy and he wore a big flat cap." (13)

(M B)

The Barrick children's favourite shop was Daisy's Store in Sunnyside Road near the footbridge over the railway. The shop *"was her front room – she just used to pull the window open and there was this little Aladdin's cave with all sorts of things ... We used to go in there with our pocket-money, because for sixpence in the old money you used to come home with a lovely lot of sweets: liquorice strings, wagon wheels, and of course she'd have one or two useful things like aspirins, cigarettes, tobacco ..."* *"Jamboree bags were what we used to buy, didn't we, with all the selections in there, sweets and a little toy. That used to be a firm favourite."* (5 and 4)

This was where Stephen Knight used to buy his *"Park Drive cigarettes, even when under age!"*

Bridge Stores, on the corner of Bridge Hill and Sunnyside, had sacks of flour and rice from which they would weigh out the amount the customer required. They also had *"sugar in blue bags and big tins of biscuits with glass lids"* as well as sweets and comics. (18)

Mrs Brown and the Whitbreads preferred Service Stores, which was half-way up Bower Hill, near the Gas Works: *"That was a lovely little shop ... They sold everything there ... It was a complete grocery shop ... You never had to go into Epping, you could just go in there, and they'd even deliver it for you – they had bikes."* (12 and 11)

One of those delivery bikes was ridden by Stephen Knight. He worked for both Service Stores and for Bridge Stores, on the corner of Bridge Hill and Sunnyside Road, which were owned by the same people, the Reeves. Straight after school from 4.30 to 6. 30 and all day Saturday, he *"used to deliver groceries on an old trade bike - an Elswick Hopper."* There was a rack over the front wheel which took four big cardboard boxes, and sometimes two more stacked on top. His round included Fiddlers Hamlet, Charles Street and, later, The Orchards. It was, he recalls, *"jolly hard work."* (17)

The trades-boys were not the only ones on bikes.
"Occasionally, in the season, the onion-sellers used to come round from France, with strings of onions on the handlebars." (5)
And there was *"a man on a bicycle with a box, selling ice-creams."* (2)

In the early days, some of the deliveries were still being made by horse and cart. Doreen Grimwade's husband, for example, was briefly the rounds-man for Simmons the Baker. His area was South Epping and Theydon Bois.
"He'd do all his booking with the horse plodding home. He'd be sitting there in this two-wheeled cart and the horse would stumble. Of course, he would shoot out and all his money would roll about the pavement! I came out of the cart <u>again</u> today, he'd say, stupid horse!" (3)

On Mondays, *"there used to be a lot of horse-riders go up, when they used to ride round from the country to the market."* (11)

Angela Wilkins remembers that, as well as the bicycling ice-cream man, *"two ladies used to come round with a horse and a nice cart, selling ice-cream. I used to take a carrot out for the horse."*
It was the ice-cream itself that Joyce Whitbread recalls: *"Penny Wall's! You used to pay a penny for these long Toblerone-shaped ices. What <u>did</u> they call them? Fruity drops, wasn't it, or something like that."*
Later on, lollies and cones were served from the van driven by Mr Dodd, who lived on the estate.

Occasionally, the rag-and-bone-man would drive slowly past, ringing a bell. If anyone came out with a bundle of rags, *"he *used to weigh the bag on a great big hook."* Sometimes he would give the children a penny, or a goldfish! (4 and 5)

More regularly, there was *"Bunny the Butcher, we used to call him. He always drove a white van and he would always bring sweets. He would turn up, usually on a Friday, and he would open the back of his van with all the baskets of different things."* (4) (One family chose not to have their meat delivered. During the summer, they'd noticed rather a lot of flies around one particular van, which put them off. From then on, they nick-named that delivery-man "Flyblow!")

Then there was *"Bill the Baker ... He used to come several times a week delivering fresh bread and cakes."* (5)

"We used to have a greengrocer, a butcher and a fishmonger. It was a good service. You never had to go out shopping – they'd come to you!" (11 and 12)
The greengrocer's van belonged to Mr Durban and called every Saturday. (13)

All the little shops (apart from Janet's Pantry, mentioned in the next chapter) survived until the post-prefab years, but as with so many small businesses, the rise of the supermarkets coupled with the growth of car ownership proved a lethal combination. (Dingley's, in its new guise of Allnutts Stores, still survives, probably because it retained the local Post Office. However, the Post Office is now, in 2008, under threat of closure.) The area was luckier than some, for in the UK as a whole, the number of "independent grocery convenience stores" *halved* between 1950 and 1960, dropping from 265,000 to 130,000, and had halved again by 1980. (fd) Today, corner shops are few and far between.

For many years, the number of families at Stewards Green who had a car could be counted on one hand. Two of the earliest were "Sparks" the Electrician and Ken Whitbread the

Photographer, probably because both had to cart equipment about for their work. So little traffic came round the loop that children played in the street as well as on the green. Indeed, one of J K's treasured photographs is of her 4-year-old son *sitting* in the *middle* of the road. The 1954 photo of Stephen Knight in his toy car (on page 61) shows just one parked car in the background. His father could drive, but chose to hire a car when necessary (mainly for family holidays) rather than buy one.

Despite the lack of traffic, several parents preferred to walk their children to Theydon Garnon School (just north of Fiddlers Hamlet.)
"There never has been a footpath from here down to where the little school was, so, you know what children are, take your eyes off them for a minute and whoomph, they're gone, so I would never let him go to school on his own." (12)

In 1954, the Council thought it necessary to put up four garages for the estate, which were quickly snapped up.
Doreen Grimwade, working full time as a teacher, bought her own car that year. *"Matilda! She was a wonderful car! She was made of aluminium. She was an Austin Ruby coupé."*

"Matilda" in front of the garages. (courtesy Doreen Grimwade)

Later, Mrs Grimwade got a bank loan of £25 in order to put up a little garage in the corner of her garden:
"It was made of asbestos and wood and you screwed it together. We had it up on bricks so that it didn't sink into the mud ... and we used to have a mop-head hanging up so that I didn't drive out of the back of it!"

When, in the mid 1960s, the prefabs were dismantled and the new houses and bungalows built, every house was given a car porch, and twenty garages were also provided. In the new millennium, one of the major changes noticed by the residents is the increase in traffic: People feel that they can't walk the lanes any more because of *"all the cars hare-braining it to the station" and* beyond. (8)

The Stewards Green estate was following the national trends. Statistics from the Department for Transport show that in 1950, only 14% of households had a car. By 1966, that had risen to around 40%, still only 4 out of every 10 households. Now, there are 10 times as many cars as there were in the 1950s, a figure probably exceeding 21 million! Almost 8 out of 10 households have a car! (dft)

Chapter Six

Leisure and Play

The feature of the estate that seemed to delight everybody was The Green. It was *"a lovely green centre ... the children could come out of their back gates and play."* (12)
They rode their bikes or pedal cars up and down, pushed dolls' prams round, skipped, played hopscotch, tag or jacks, and "let's pretend." There were seasons for marbles, conkers or hula hoops. The annual cut was the signal for making dens out of the loose grass. (18) Sometimes parents organised games, or football matches. (14) So popular was The Green that children from further down Stewards Green Road and from Allnutts Road would come to play there. (18)

They rode their bikes or pedal cars up and down. (B and O K.)

The children were also in and out of each other's gardens:
"When my son had a birthday, I loaded up the table with all sorts of things that children would like, left the back door open and they all came through the wire [fence] at the back, because they all knew one another. I can remember one little boy came tearing in, biscuit in both hands, rushed out again!

They were all playing on that field, but they came in for the food and drink." (7)
"We'd always got a houseful of kids." (10)

"They all played together nicely" (12) on the whole, and the mums *"used to keep an eye on each other's,"* (4) but of course, now and again there would be mishaps or mischief. For example, J K's son, aged about 5 or 6, had been playing outside when he called out, *""Mum, you come and see my fountain." He had hit a water pipe with a wooden hammer!"*

Another instance: one summer's day Pam Barrick and her friends were playing at having a birthday party in the garden and had decorated a "pretend" cake with real candles. When these were lit, the dry grass caught fire and soon the edge of the field was alight. A fire engine had to be called. (On at least one other occasion, the farmer's stubble-burning got out of control, also resulting in the arrival of the Fire Brigade. (15))

Mary Batley and/or her brother broke their prefab windows with balls more than once, and she suspects that this was why their next-door-neighbour had a high hedge!
"When my mum left work at St Margaret's Hospital she would go into a shop and buy a pane of glass. She would walk home from the town to the prefabs with a pane of glass under her arm!"

"There were several harum-scarum little boys," one of whom *"used to collect up all the little tiny conkers and small potatoes"* (7) as ammunition for his catapult. One day Peggy Killick's husband was painting in front of an open window. The boy fired a potato *"and, you'd never believe it, it shot right through the open window and how it didn't hit Jack's nose – it must have almost touched – it went whizzing through! I shall never forget the way he chased after that boy! He never caught him, of course!"*

Pulling faces at grown-ups using the telephone box, quarrelling in a sand-pit, allegations of taking or breaking someone's toy, big ones pushing little ones over – such things sometimes led to the cry *"I'll tell your Mum!"* (3) Then there might be a little bit of *"argy-bargy"* until the parents sorted it out.

But these were minor squabbles. Essentially, people remember that the children played well together and that The Green was *"a happy place."* (12)

(M B)

The surrounding countryside wasn't merely a useful resource supplying additional food and fuel (as described in Chapter Three.) It also provided a playground for young and old alike and lifted people's spirits. *"It was an idyllic spot. We had such a lot of wildlife, so many birds and rabbits and hedgehogs."* (3)

Two of the men *"loved their fishing and they had permission to go to a nice lake."* (5)
Close by, near the four cottages, the pond (now filled in) used to harbour *"the lovely big protected newts."* (3) The Knights would take their boys fishing there. A walk across the field to look at the pigs was a favourite with Len Butcher's children.

Talking of animals, one boy, Colin Livett, brought a dog home that he'd found tied in a sack that was lying in a ditch. *"Mum fell in love with the dog and wanted to call him Laddy. He had a lovely shiny black coat with a white patch on the front and a white tip on his tail. He was a Collie dog."* (13)

Colin also rescued an orphaned baby rabbit, built a hutch and tried to rear it. But some other lads took a more robust "country" attitude. Pre-myxomatosis, the rabbit population had reached enormous proportions and in 1954 the Government had passed the Pests Act, designating areas for rabbit clearance. A few years on, Stephen Knight and his two friends were happy to lend a hand!
"The highlight of the year for us was the harvesting of the crops." The farmer *"used to cut the corn round and round, which would push the rabbits into the centre."* At the last moment they would try to dash away *"and then we would despatch them with sticks."* (17)

"My son was a wanderer," according to J K. He'd tell her, *"Mum, I'm off over the front fields,"* and would set off to search for birds' nests. It was common in those days for small boys to collect birds' eggs, but he was told not to touch.

Val Grant collected caterpillars and ladybirds in jars, climbed trees and, on one memorable Monday, fell in the pond. When she got home, covered in mud, she was put, fully clothed, into the copper!

Several residents mentioned country walks as an enjoyable family activity. Phil Berry listed *"strolls in adjoining fields"* as his main leisure-time pursuit. Peggy Killick called her husband *"a roamer of fields"* and a regular route for them was *"up Flux's Lane and round, out in the fields at the back."* The Theydon Garnon area was popular with the Browns, while the Thakes would walk or cycle to Coopersale and back, or up Stonards Hill.

On their blackberrying or sloe-picking forays, the Barrick girls would sometimes cycle up to the Tawney Common area, and then they would stop at the Mole Trap public house. *"We'd perhaps sit outside, not with a shandy because we weren't old enough, but with a lemonade and a packet of crisps, to have a little rest and revive before we did the return journey."*

Another place they often called at was "Janet's Pantry" at Fiddlers Hamlet.
"If we'd been out on our bikes or for a walk with Mum and Dad we'd quite often end up having a little sit-down and got our breath there. They had a large paved area with wrought iron and wooden furniture, and they had double doors that opened up. You used to go in and place your order for afternoon tea or a cold drink ... They were lovely ladies and the garden was pretty." (5)

Val Flack, née Grant, also remembers lemonade and crisps. On a nice day she would walk along the lane with her Mum and Dad to the Merry Fiddlers, admiring the celandines that were flowering in the ditches. Then she would sit in the pub garden with her treat. (18)

There were also *organised* activities for the children locally, such as the Scouts and Cubs in the Hut at the bottom of Flux's Lane, and the Guides, the Girls' Life Brigade, and the Sunday School, who met in the hall in Allnutts Road.

The nearest Scout troop had originally been in Kendal Avenue, which was the group that J K's son belonged to.

Soon after the young Reverend Crellin arrived at Theydon Garnon Church in 1958, he approached Ken and Joyce Whitbread and asked if they would be willing to start a new troop. They agreed and did a six-week course at the Scouts' Gillwell Park headquarters. But getting suitable premises was more difficult to organise. First a shed was bought from the Gas Works for £25 – it took them a month to clean it out. Then there were protracted negotiations in order to buy, rather than rent, the field on the corner of Flux's Lane. (Eventually, it was donated to them.) Later, an ex-Army hut was purchased which had to be collected from Chester.

At its strongest, the 1st Theydon Garnon troop consisted of 100 boys from the surrounding roads. The Whitbreads estimate that almost half of the eligible lads from the prefabs belonged at one time. As well as weekly meetings, regular camps were organised during the summer, at Easter and at Whitsun for up to 15 boys at a time, travelling as far afield as Suffolk, Yorkshire, Wales and Scotland.

The first Scottish trip nearly didn't happen, because there were insufficient funds to hire a mini-bus for a fortnight. Ken Whitbread was determined not to let the boys down. When he was driving past the garage on The Plain he noticed that there was a *"van out there, it was painted red with all white flower-power stuff on it! Students had just come back from the Sahara with it."* Ken bought it, *"parked it in front of the prefab, got a roller and some Dulux paint and we painted it white. That was on a Thursday. On the Saturday at 6 o'clock in the morning we had twelve boys out there, with all their gear on, to go camping in Scotland. The parents all came to see us off. They said, "Ken, give us a ring when you break down and we'll come and pick you up!" So at half past six that night I phoned them. They said, "Ha! How far have you got?" I said, "At the moment, the boys are all sitting down at the side of Loch Lomond, having sausage, mash and beans!" They wouldn't believe it!"* (11)

"When we were coming back from Scotland, all we could hear was vhee-vhee-vhee-vhee-vhee! I said to Ken, "There's something wrong with the van," so we pulled into a lay-by. The boys had filled the van, absolutely filled it, with grasshoppers!" (12)

There were also local weekends – Mr Power, for example, the farmer near the Mole Trap, would let them camp in a field. On one occasion, the West Essex Gazette reported that, "28 cubs had their first taste of life under canvas when they went for an all day camp."

Joyce Whitbread with the Cubs (K W)

Mary Batley remembers very clearly the time she was invited to go to the Girls' Life Brigade by her friend Carol Dodd. They would have been about nine years old.

"She looked nice in her navy blue uniform. She wore a tartan tie and a blue beret with a blue badge with GLB in red letters, and also she wore white gloves ... There was a young girl there who was playing the piano and we all marched to the music. I remember Carol singing On the Good Ship Lollipop!"

Being a member of the choir at Theydon Garnon Church, as Stephen Knight was, involved a two-hour rehearsal every Thursday evening and attendance at both Matins and Evensong on a Sunday. Sometimes the choir-boys would also sing at weddings and, occasionally, at funerals. Before the electric organ was installed, the bellows had to be pumped by hand: now and again *"a long oak handle used to pop out at the wrong moment!"* Stephen really enjoyed it and became head choir-boy.

In the early days, for many of the adults the constraints of jobs, child-rearing and house-work, not to mention a lack of funds, meant that leisure pursuits tended to be extensions of necessary activities. But vegetable-growing and gardening, blackberry-picking and jam-making etc were for many people a pleasure, not just a chore. Several residents, for instance, joined the Horticultural Society that met in Coopersale.

Some of the men would go for an occasional drink at The Spotted Dog, Ivy Chimneys, or The Merry Fiddlers at Fiddlers Hamlet. *"I would occasionally go down to The Merry Fiddlers with my father-in-law for a quick one on a Sunday, with the instructions that our dinner would be on the table at 1 o'clock and don't be late!"* (8)
On the whole, people didn't indulge in this way – money was too tight.

Until 1954 Epping had its own cinema, The Empire. Four families mentioned that they used to go there. *"Occasionally, Dad would babysit, and Mum and one or two of the neighbours would go to the cinema, to give them a bit of a break."* (5)

Because J K's mother used to look after her little boy at the weekends, she and her husband went further afield, to the Stratford Empire to see a revue, or even to the West End: *"not a lot of young wives got the chance to do that."*

Two or three of the residents, including Mr Barrick, belonged to a charitable organisation called "The Water Buffaloes."

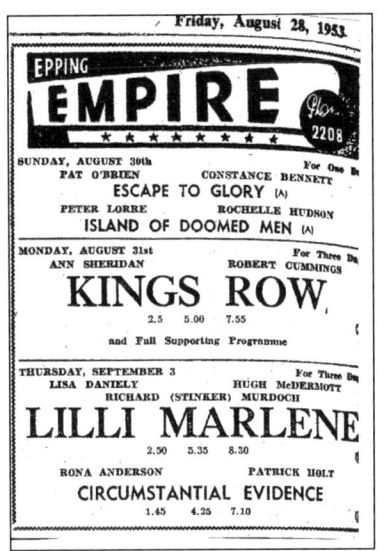

They would meet once a week in a hall attached to The White Hart public house. *"The men used to play table-tennis and darts to have a bit of social life,"* (5) and they also did fund-raising events. With the money raised, they would provide parties or outings for the children, to the sea-side or to Whipsnade Zoo, for example, once or twice a year.

Mr Wally Brown is remembered as being *"good to the people of the prefabs – he would arrange coach trips twice a year to Margate or Ramsgate or Southend to see the lights ... On the coach they would sing songs – "I would like to go a-wandering" and "Knees up Mother Brown!"* (13)

The local newspapers regularly carried reports and results from the Caged Birds Societies. Ken Whitbread was an enthusiast. In his garden he had two aviaries, one for British birds and one for budgerigars and canaries – almost 100 birds altogether.

"When we used to show them, we used to have to bath them. Then Ken used to wrap them round with cotton wool and lay

them in front of the fire to dry. We had four cats, and not <u>once</u> did any of the cats attempt to touch them!" (12)
One year, one of his budgies won Best in Show at Olympia.

No doubt there were many more hobbies, games and pastimes pursued on the estate by both adults and children – this chapter can only scratch the surface.

Chapter Seven

Event and Characters

The first major occasion that looms large in the memories of the residents is Queen Elizabeth 11's Coronation in June 1953.

No-one I've spoken to can quite remember who was responsible for the Stewards Green children's party, except that it was "the Mums." It was very well attended, as shown by Ken Whitbread's photo.

(K W)

In the January, the West Essex Gazette had produced a Gift Book "suitable for very young children and also for the 8 – 15 age group." They suggested it would be a "useful Coronation present." These were offered for a nominal charge to organisers of children's parties on a first-come-first-served basis. Either "the Mums" were not impressed with the book, or perhaps they applied late, because the gifts that are remembered are a mug and a coin. (6)

"Each household provided a plate of food of some description – sandwiches, biscuits, cakes," (3) and these were set out on long trestle tables.

Games were played, but what was most commented on was the Fancy Dress Competition.

Mary Batley née Livett remembers that her aunt *"came to the prefab that day to curl my hair, and my mum dressed me as a fairy. She made my dress and wings from white paper, and my crown and wand from white-and-silver-paper. I came second and "Dolly Duster" came first."*

"The Queen of Hearts who stole some tarts" was Pam Barrick's costume.

"We dressed all the kids up in red, white and blue, we made all these costumes ..." (3)

(D G)

In the evening, many people went up to the Fair in Stonards Hill, where all the rides were free. Then *"we all watched fireworks and we sang God Save the Queen."* (13)

Mary and Mrs Livett with Mrs Hawes at the Fair. (M B)

It sounds as if it was a really enjoyable day, despite the poor weather.

In March 1954 there was a very serious incident:
Mrs Parrish's son Roy was a keen motor-cyclist *"and in the shed he kept a 2-gallon can of petrol. Mrs Parrish came home and wanted to light the fire but found that the wood was damp. She went out to the shed, picked up what she thought was paraffin ... it dripped along ... She tipped some of it on the fire. The result was that the place went up very quickly."* (8 and 9)

"I was at home and I heard a funny noise, and when I looked out, there was no roof, it was just a mass of flame!" (7)

Mary Livett, who was about seven years old at the time, was waiting for her mother at the end of the prefabs by the main road.
"As I looked up, I could see a puff of smoke and lots of people standing at the top of the road. They were nowhere near the burning prefab." (13)
This was because the corrugated asbestos-sheet roofing *"exploded like firework explosions – it cracked and flew and shattered – it fractured into fragments."* (8)

Never-the-less, Mr Sewell, (or Mrs Sewell, according to the press,) a neighbour, *"walked into the burning prefab, rescued Mrs Parrish and saved her life,"* (13 and WEG) but her pet bird and all her possessions were lost.

Meanwhile, Mrs Livett was on her way home from work.
"She got as far as the Castle at Bower Hill. She could see the flames and thought it was <u>her</u> prefab and that I was inside ... When she arrived, she passed out. Mrs Ratcliffe gave her a glass of water, and then she came round and went home to bed." (13)
"Oh, it did frighten the children, all of them, it really did, because it went up, whoosh!" (7)

The adults were badly shaken, too, realising how a simple mistake could prove catastrophic.

"It just goes to show you, when you see something like that, to take care." (7)

"It made people think, because she wasn't insured, and nor was anyone else on the estate. We thought, all your goods, how do you replace them? I immediately took out a Fire Insurance." (8)

Another result was that *"after the fire the GPO put a telephone box at the top of the road, and it still stands there today."* (13)

The bungalow was never rebuilt, but four garages were erected on the site.

From an accidental fire, to a controlled one! November 5th was celebrated yearly.

"There'd be an enormous bonfire made at Guy Fawkes Night, on the middle of the Green." (3)

"It used to go way up, oh it used to be terrific!" (7)

This proved useful for the tenants, who could get rid of household and garden rubbish.

"We'd all have our own fireworks in the gardens, and we'd have parkin and jacket potatoes and toffee-apples. Then they'd all get handed around – if you had a few toffee-apples left over, you'd hand them over the fence, that sort of thing." (3)

The fathers would keep a close eye on the children, in case any burning branches tumbled from the top of the huge pile.

"There'd be an enormous bonfire on the middle of the Green." (M B)

On one occasion, two boys (who had better remain nameless!) had been the main builders of the bonfire, so they decided they had the right to light it themselves, but did so on November 4th! And so *"the children of the prefabs had fireworks but no bonfire!"* (13)

The bonfire would often *"stay burning on the ground, just a low glow, for days. Some of the local lads would be out there blowing it, getting it going again, putting a little grass on it, as boys will, and sometimes kept it going for a week, until some parent that was a bit worried would go out with a bucket of water and make sure it was definitely out ...We used to have a lovely Bonfire Night back then."* (7)

In September 1958 a tremendous storm, rumoured to be the tail-end of a hurricane, struck Southern England, including Stewards Green.

"Torrential rain came down from the fields. We opened the back door and it was almost coming in ... The whole of the yard was flooded, the garden was flooded, the sewers had backed up and the man-hole covers had lifted. There was effluent all floating around – we were sweeping it away with brooms." (8)

"It had been raining heavily for some time, and then after dark we heard voices outside. On investigating, we found a couple of neighbours trying to divert a flood-stream of water which was pouring off the fields at the back of the estate. I went and got my shovel and joined the others trying to build a bank of earth to divert it from the prefabs, but it was rather a hopeless task. My wife then came out and told me the water was getting in – several inches covered the floor in my daughter's bedroom. She was asleep in her cot and the bedside light was on – the flex was trailing on the floor under water! ...It took weeks to dry out and to get rid of the smell – floorboards had to come up. We later built an earth barrier along the bottom of our gardens." (15)

The Housing Department weren't very helpful, apparently. No-one seemed to get *"Council back-up,"* (15) and it was a long time before *"the Council chap eventually came down. He was surprised – he hadn't believed us when we told him about the sewers."* (8)

The man should *not* have been surprised, because way back in April, the Public Health Committee had discussed "the flooding problem ... after sudden heavy rain," in the Brook Road and Stewards Green area. A report suggested that a new, larger sewer should be installed, but because of the cost, it was decided that "no action could be taken at the present." This angered one Councillor, who said, "I have seen this water gushing out like a water-spout ... I think the matter is serious, and I think it will get more serious." (Mins and WEG)

He was right! (A wider sewer was eventually put in.)

That September night was etched into the memories of church-goers from Dovercourt and Theydon Garnon. Members of the Dovercourt congregation had travelled up to see their former curate, Mr Howard Crellin, installed as Rector at All Saints Church. After his induction, everyone set off for the reception at Allnutts Institute.

"We were victims of the storm and spent most of the evening wading through floods," wrote David Pringle in the West Essex Gazette.

"The water at Theydon Garnon was deep, but it had nothing on Stewards Green Road. It had turned into a river." In order to get their coach through, several men had to push abandoned cars out of the centre of the road. "In places the water reached my thighs and broken twigs and debris floated past." (WEG)

When they eventually reached Allnutts it was almost 11pm.
" "The most eventful induction ever," said 28-year-old Rev Howard Crellin as he sat with his feet in a bath of hot water," trying to wash the mud off." (WEG)
Fifty years later, Rev Crellin still clearly remembers that day. (16)

As well as the problematic sewers, agricultural changes had almost certainly contributed towards the flooding:
"When the farmers started making large fields to entertain the combine harvesters, they filled in lots of ditches, they filled in lots of ponds ..." (8)
This meant that in the face of extreme weather conditions, *"the field ditches and road drains were "unfit for purpose," as they say nowadays."* (15)

Len Butcher has another weather-related tale.
"During the hard winter of 1963, we had kicked our hot-water bottle out of the bed onto the floor after it had cooled. On picking it up in the morning, we found it full of slushy ice!" Bbrrr!

The snow and ice were unrelenting. On the front page of January's West Essex Gazette, Ken Whitbread, by now Assistant District Commissioner for Epping and Ongar, put out a call for all Cubs to "help the old folk by doing their shopping and gathering their wood."

Now for some "characters."
Some of the occasional visitors to the estate could seem alarming to the children.
There was a *"man in a flat cap who came round with plants and big pots. If I saw him coming with his plants, I used to run a mile! I don't know why, he used to frighten me, walking around with a box of plants, carrying it on his head!"* (2)

There was *"a tramp who lived from time to time in the old barn near the Four Cottages. We gave him a wide berth as he was quite frightening to us children,"* because he seemed to appear suddenly and silently in odd places. (17) Mrs Barrick would often give these itinerant workmen a bite to eat. (5)

Sometimes a family of travellers *"used to camp, with just a canvas tilt for cover, on the footpath between the Four Cottages."* (17) If gypsies came to the door selling wooden pegs or heather, Mrs Barrick would never turn them away, holding the old country belief that to do so would bring bad luck. (5)

One of the more welcome visitors was Dr Korte.
JK had particular reason to be grateful to him. Her son had caught measles and was *"dreadfully bad. I'd got him in his little back bedroom with the curtains pulled, like they tell you ... That night, I said to my husband, "Whatever's that noise?"* Her son was gasping for breath. Dr Korte came straight away, diagnosed pneumonia and then organised hospital admission, which wasn't easy as the local isolation hospitals were all full. Finally he spoke reassuringly to the boy: *"Will you go over to*

my little hospital for a little while ... it's ever so nice over there ..."

"He was a lovely man, I liked him a lot because he was so nice with the kids ... he had time for them, which not all doctors have." (6)

Peggy Killick's daughter was taken ill suddenly on a Sunday. Peggy ran all the way up to Epping Place to fetch the doctor and he immediately stopped what he was doing and drove her back to Stewards Green.

He took time to listen to the adults' worries, too.
"I got a little bit depressed. Dr Korte was wonderful ... He said, "You know what you want to do, fill a flask, make some sandwiches, go out with the ladies that are potato-picking ... spend the day with everybody else. You'll have a good laugh and you'll enjoy it." (7) This prescription worked!

Another popular visitor was Rev Howard Crellin, who had had such an eventful arrival in his new parish.
"Our vicar used to come and visit us – he was a wonderful vicar! He used to come up here in his old wellies to have a chat. He sat there talking one night and he said, "I think we ought to start a Scout Group. Are you prepared to do it?""
(12)

"He encouraged all the kids – the older kids as well, who'd left school and were standing on street corners smoking away – he encouraged them to come to church."
As well as getting the lads to join the choir, he also took them to London to help with giving food to down-and-outs. Because a few boys were struggling with maths, he tutored them, and he encouraged them to join a savings scheme. (8)

"Mr Crellin was a fantastic rector - always had time for everyone and not at all aloof."(17) For instance, *"He would go to the pub and have a drink with you."* (8)

In the summer of 1959, Mr Crellin bought the Church minibus, which he usually drove himself. He would collect members of the choir and congregation (the main stopping-place was the Stewards Green Road and Bower Hill junction (WEG)) and then return them home after the service. If he passed a parishioner on some other business, he would still offer them a lift. (8)

At the Church's annual meeting in 1964, it was revealed that the average Sunday attendance was up by half, to almost 200. ""It is good to see such a cross-section of the parish interested in the church," Rev Crellin said." (WEG)

"He was the inspiration behind Theydon Garnon's good attendance – he <u>made</u> Theydon Garnon." (8)

(Other church-goers on the estate attended St John's in the High Street or St Alban's in Coopersale.)

Among the residents themselves were one or two who stood out for some reason.
One young woman, for example, cut quite a dash and impressed the younger children with her "Teddy Girl" style:
"She always had nice clothes, she looked like a model and she was a lovely girl." (13)

On a less pleasant note, there was for a while a Peeping Tom, who was probably also the person who stole women's underwear from washing-lines! Luckily, he moved from the estate quite soon.
And one woman was famed for her bad language: *"She had a terrible mouth on her - tongue a yard long and forked!"*

Other people are remembered because of their slightly eccentric behaviour. For example, an elderly man always knelt to cut his front lawn with scissors; two middle-aged sisters used to take their ginger cat for a walk on a lead. (7)

These ladies were the first on the estate to have a TV, and invited their neighbours' little girl in to watch "Little Grey Rabbit" every Friday. They would also give any spare rations to their neighbours, so they are remembered mainly for their kindness. (18)

The stylish Teddy Girl. (M B)

Chapter Eight

The End of the Line

All the prefabs built under the Temporary Housing Programme had been intended as a short-term solution to the immediate post-war housing shortage. They had only been expected to last for ten years. But as most designs were proving more durable than that, and as Council-house waiting lists carried on growing, prefabs continued in service right across the country. Epping Urban District Council agreed to extend the life of Stewards Green Estate for a further five years, until 1961.

Meanwhile, Epping was slowly spreading. In the late 1950s, private houses were built from the bottom of Bower Hill along Stewards Green Road, which necessitated the re-numbering of the prefabs. A couple of years later, Stewards Close was erected.

During 1959, Epping Urban District Council drew up its Housing Programme plans.
In the coming few years the Council decided to build:
37 houses for tenants who were currently in sub-standard accommodation; 30 bungalows for elderly couples; 82 houses for people on the waiting-list; and "permanent structures" for the 39 households at Stewards Green. (WEG)

Problems began when someone checked the Town Development Plan. This had originally been drawn up in 1937, showing how, in the future, different parts of Epping should be zoned. Areas were designated for residential, commercial, light industrial and recreational use. The plan was amended in 1951, but it completely ignored the prefabs – the estate site was shown as an empty field, shaded to indicate public open space.

By 1961, opposition to the Council's plan was taking shape. At the Epping and District Preservation Society's annual meeting, "there were some sharp exchanges." The chairman opposed the redevelopment on the grounds that, "It is a matter of nibbling a bit of the Green Belt *here* and nibbling a bit *here* until there is nothing left." At least two members supported the scheme, pointing out that the site was one of few already owned by the Council, and that there were over 100 people on the waiting list. However, the Society voted against.

On April 24th 1961, a Public Inquiry was held by an Inspector from the Ministry of Housing and Local Government. A large petition protesting about the redevelopment was handed in by the misleadingly-named "Stewards Green and District Residents' Association," which represented *no-one* from the *estate*, but plenty from the local private houses. This petition was countered by one from the prefab residents themselves. It had been organised by Mr Wally Brown and contained 71 signatures – every single husband, wife and young adult living in the Tarran bungalows.

Reading between the lines of the Gazette's report on the debate, the main objections from the Stewards Green and District Residents' Association were that the proposed two-storey buildings would interrupt the views and (possibly) lower the property values of the Stewards Close houses. (It is intriguing to learn that the Gazette's editor lived there.) The Epping and District Preservation Society argued against using four acres of Green Belt land and losing public open space.

After rebutting these points in detail, Mr Harry Mead, Epping's Surveyor, summed up the Council's defence like this:

"One, the site has been used for housing for fifteen years. Secondly, there will be no spoiling of the amenities by the type of building that is envisaged for the site. And thirdly, there is plenty of other land for recreational purposes." (WEG)

Four months later, the Gazette carried the headline:
"Council wins Battle of Prefabs – BUT"
The Inspector had allowed the redevelopment, provided that the buildings on the north-west side of the estate were bungalows with low-pitched roofs. Another requirement was that the ten acres to the north should be a recreation ground.[*]

It may have been during this time of controversy that some Stewards Green residents became aware of a change in attitude towards the estate. In the early days, *"I think people thought we were very fortunate, because such a lot of people were having to cram in with their families."* (7) Friends would come round to admire the kitchen and its "mod cons" and the prefab-dwellers felt privileged.

Now, some felt that, *"We were commoners, put it that way."* (12)
"They didn't want us here, I remember that very well." (9)
"The trouble was that all the other property down there was privately owned, so therefore very middle class. And we were, of course, a Council estate, so there was a feeling of them and us." (3) (It should be noted that not all residents reacted like this.)

During the re-development, the Council had quite a juggling act on its hands, because demolition and building work were going on side by side.
"They started knocking down the prefabs from [the western] end and re-housing the people from that end." (8)

---

[*] This land has never been used for that purpose, despite the best efforts of the residents. In 1969, after one or two tenants had complained about ball games on the new Green, Bob Knight organised a petition calling for a playing field. (Mins) In 1974, the 13-year-old Elizabeth Thake and her friends Beverley Green and Pauline Jones did the same, but to no avail. (Ind)

The first few tenants were moved temporarily into the Springfield, Beaconfield or Centre Drive areas so that their prefabs could be removed. Joyce Whitbread was astonished at how quickly they were dismantled. *"Houses were put up, and then the next prefabs taken down – it was well organised."* (11)

There were, however, some unexpected hitches. At least one resident refused point-blank to be re-housed next to a particular family. The situation was discussed in a Housing Committee meeting, and it was decided to accommodate people's preferences as far as possible. (Mins)

One or two people were moved for a short time from their own prefab to a vacated one, but most were able to move straight to their new house or bungalow. *"We just did it between us. We didn't get Removals, we just brought everything down bit by bit."* (2)

The Thakes' prefab, which had been used as the site office, was the last to come down. It was the end of an era.

People had mixed feelings. Some were surprised by the unusual design of the re-build, while others *"just thought it was a nice new house."* (1)

"I didn't want the prefabs to be dismantled. I realised they had to be, but I knew that it would destroy the atmosphere of the place – it was going to change it completely and utterly." (3)

That family moved away, but those who stayed were very positive, once some teething troubles with the new houses were sorted out.

Mrs Rene Andrews, quoted in the local paper in 1967, said, "I prefer this site to any other in Epping. My family and I have lived at Stewards Green for twenty years. Before the houses were built, we lived in the old prefabs along the front. I don't feel isolated down here - in the summer it's lovely." (Ind)

Being on the edge of the countryside is still part of the estate's appeal today.

Chapter Nine

Reflections

Of course, when people are asked to contribute to a booklet such as this, it is nearly always those with *happy* memories who come forward. But it is clear that the vast majority of residents really did enjoy living in the prefabs at Stewards Green. There was a fairly steady turn-over of tenants, as permanent houses were built and offered to them, but in the estate's first fifteen years only *eight* households actively requested a transfer, usually because of growing families.
(WEG, quoting Mr HJ Mead.)

Looking back, people remember that *"Everybody was friendly; you wouldn't pass anybody because you knew them all."* (9) But in a community of over 100 adults and children, there were bound to be varying degrees of sociability. On the one hand, *"I always used to make them welcome, anyone who came round, we always used to have a chinwag."* (7) On the other hand, one person's neighbours never spoke to her at all: *"They weren't very nice."* Most people chatted over the chain-link fences, but *"You were being nosy if you went into someone's garden."* (8) Some people preferred more privacy, such as the man who grew a tall hedge around his immaculate garden. (13)

Even the happiest of large families will have its tensions and squabbles, its rough diamonds and black sheep. Occasionally, there were allegations of wrong-doing or deep-seated disagreements between neighbours (witness the hitch during the redevelopment mentioned in the previous chapter.) But these seem to have been the exceptions.

The glue that held the community together had several components:

Firstly, several families had more than one branch on the estate –two Killicks, three Whitbreads and four Browns, for example – and many of the men were ex-pupils of St John's School, so there was a shared experience of growing up in Epping.

Secondly, people in the early years were recovering from the war and the adversities of austerity, so there was the sense of *"everybody being in the same boat."* (10))

Many had no wish to move up to the main town:
"We were country people born and bred." (9)
"I love it down here. I like being out in the country - I'm a country girl, see!" (1)

And, probably most importantly, they were nearly all bringing up young families:
"That's what brought people together, the kids." (8)

And so the combination of well-designed homes in a lovely location, plus friendly neighbours in similar circumstances, meant that most people look back at their time in the Stewards Green prefabs with great affection.

The Stewards Green Prefabs 1946 - 1965

"It was an idyllic time of our lives."

"I'd go back tomorrow, and so would a lot of other people, believe me!"

"Lovely little places!"

(K W)

1, 2, 3. Mrs Whitbread with Patrick and Paul
4. Mrs Killick
5, 6. Mr and Mrs Parrish
7. Mrs Jackson
8. Mrs Doe
9. Mrs Wren
10. Mrs Seymour
11. Mrs Harris
12. Mr O'Neil
13. Mrs Hawes
14. Mrs Livett
15. Mr Doe
16. Mrs Brown
17. John Ratcliffe
18, 19. Alan and David Gould
20, 21. Valerie and Christine Hammond
22. Terry Harris
23. Colin Livett
24. Michael Brown
25. Brian Wren
26. Angela Brown
27. Jenny Andrews
28. Stephen Killick
29. Val Grant
30. Peter Wren
31. Anton Hawes
32. Marylyn Barrick

(Thanks to Mrs Sylvia Brown and Mrs Angela Wilkins, and Mrs Val Flack for the identifications. – pages 90 and 92)

(K W)

-92-

1. Sally O'Neil
2. Freddie Brown
3. Diana Andrews
4. Mrs Gould
5. Mr Hammond
6. Mr Brown
7. Mrs Brown
8. Mrs Brown
9. Miss Austin
10. Mrs Whitbread
11. Sandra Jackson
12. Mrs Sewell
13. Mrs Boydell
14. Mr Brown
15. Mrs O'Neil
16. Mrs Hammond
17. Mrs Brown
18. Mrs Stephens
19. Mr Gould
20. Mr Dodd
21. Mrs Killick
22. Mrs Dodd
23. Mrs Barrick
24. Mrs Berry
25. Mr Collins
26. Michael Stephens
27. Carole Brown
28. Pam Barrick
29. Keith Whitbread
30. Robert Dodd
31. Carole Dodd
32. ? Collins
33. Colin? Berry
34. David Boydell
35. Norman Brown
36. Mrs Ada Cook

References

The quotations are from

Interviews with former Stewards Green residents *

1. Sylvia Brown and
2. Angela Wilkins, her daughter.
3. Doreen Grimwade
4. June Jones and
5. Pam O'Leary, the Barrick sisters
6. JK
7. Peggy Killick
8. Bob Knight and
9. Olive Knight.
10. Ted Thake
11. Ken Whitbread and
12. Joyce Whitbread.

Letters and conversations

13. Mary Batley née Livett *
14. Phil Berry
15. Len Butcher *
16. Reverend Howard Crellin
17. Stephen Knight *
18. Val Flack née Grant *

Additional interview material from Epping residents*

19. Mary Arbon
20. Mick Arbon
21. Jessie Childs
22. Doreen Duffell
23. Edith Fairman (of Abridge)
24. Patricia Osborne
25. Stan Osborne

*These recordings and letters can be consulted at Epping Forest District Museum, by appointment.

Primary Sources

Mins: Epping Urban District Council Minutes
WEG: West Essex Gazette – Epping edition
Ind: Express and Independent – Epping edition
ArW: Air-raid Wardens' notes

Secondary sources

Books:
  a) Palaces for the People: Prefabs in Post-war Britain by Greg Stevenson. Batsford 2003
  b) Prefabs: a history of the Temporary Housing Programme by Brenda Vale. E and F N Spoon 1995
  c) The Tragedy of Spriggs Oak and The Long Range Rocket at St Margaret's Hospital by Mike Osborne. Epping Town Council 2006
  d) Epping through the eyes of Fred by Fred Brown. 1996
  e) A Penny for Biscuits by Patricia Green. (unpublished memoir in ERO.)
  f) Never Again by Peter Hennessey. Allen Lane 2006
  g) A World to Build by David Kynaston. Bloomsbury 2007

www.statistics.gov.uk
www.dft.gov.uk
www.fooddeserts.org

Further information and help was given by:

John Duffell, local historian;
Nick Hill, director of Eden Camp Museum, Malton, North Yorkshire;
Epping Forest District Museum;
Essex Record Office;
London Transport Museum;
Shirley Hawkins of Epping Forest District Council;
Carol Leach of The Forester;
Edmund Tobin of Epping Forest Guardian.